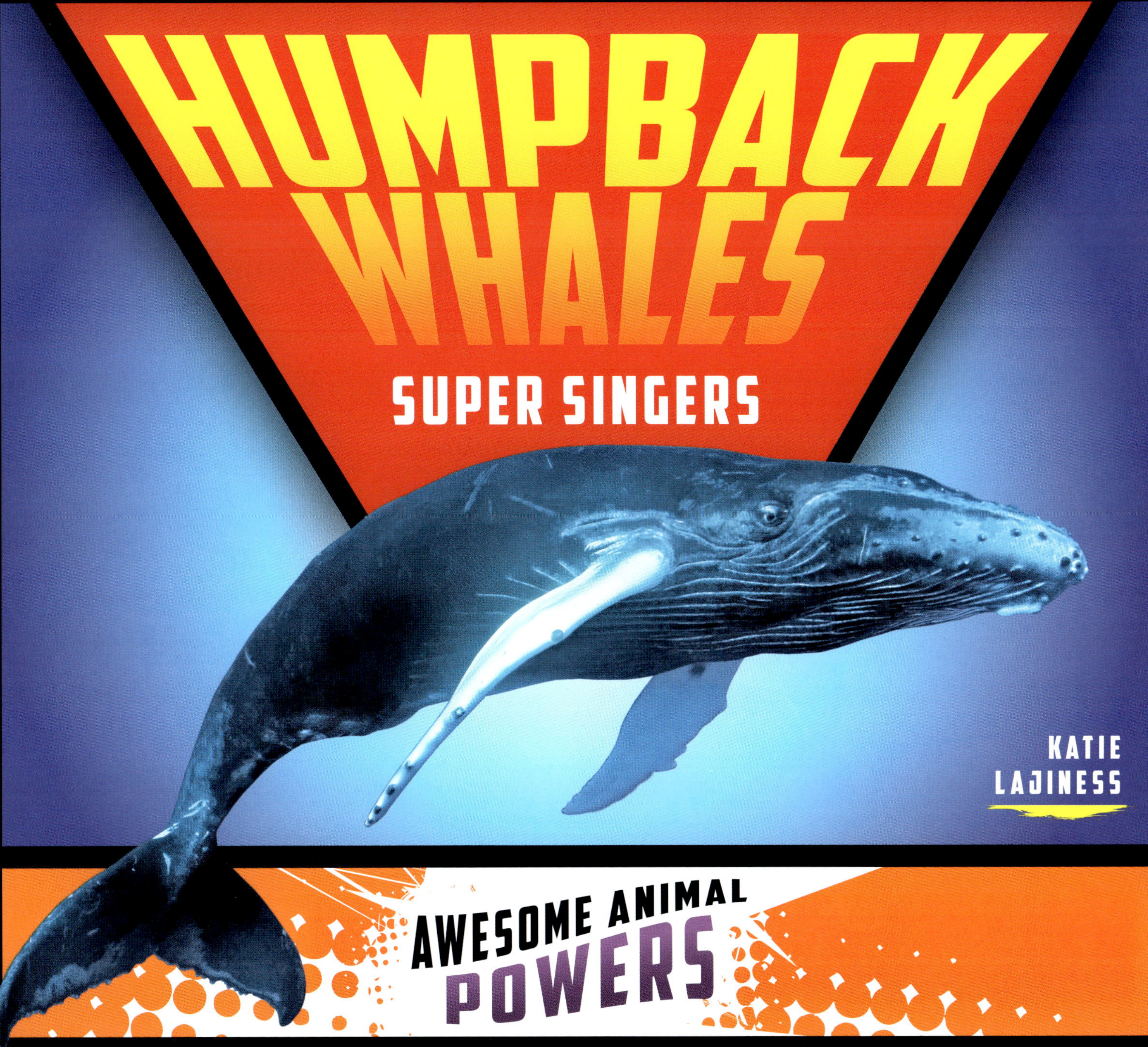
HUMPBACK WHALES
SUPER SINGERS
KATIE LAJINESS
AWESOME ANIMAL POWERS

abdopublishing.com

Published by Abdo Publishing, a division of ABDO, PO Box 398166, Minneapolis, Minnesota 55439.

Printed in the United States of America, North Mankato, Minnesota.
052018
092018

Cover Photo: imageBROKER/Alamy Stock Photo.
Interior Photos: Betty Wiley/Getty Images (p. 15); Bryce Flynn/Getty Images (p. 27); Eric Kulin/Getty Images (p. 7); evenfh/Getty Images (p. 5); Fabrice Guerin/Getty Images (pp. 19, 29); Henrik Johansson, www.shutter-life.com/Getty Images (p. 21); imageBROKER/Alamy Stock Photo (p. 30); John Warden/Getty Images (p. 23); Kerstin Meyer/Getty Images (p. 25); M Swiet Productions/Getty Images (pp. 7, 9); Olaf Kruger/Getty Images (p. 17); Rodrigo Friscione/Getty Images (p. 11).

Coordinating Series Editor: Tamara L. Britton
Contributing Editor: Jill Roesler
Graphic Design: Jenny Christensen, Erika Weldon

Library of Congress Control Number: 2017961385

Publisher's Cataloging-in-Publication Data

Names: Lajiness, Katie, author.
Title: Humpback Whales: Super singers / by Katie Lajiness.
Other titles: Super singers
Description: Minneapolis, Minnesota : Abdo Publishing, 2019. | Series: Awesome animal powers | Includes online resources and index.
Identifiers: ISBN 9781532115004 (lib.bdg.) | ISBN 9781532155727 (ebook)
Subjects: LCSH: Humpback whale--Juvenile literature. | Humpback whale--Behavior--Juvenile literature. | Whale sounds--Juvenile literature. | Animal communication--Juvenile literature.
Classification: DDC 599.51--dc23

CONTENTS

THE HUMPBACK WHALE 4

BOLD BODIES 6

THAT'S AWESOME! 8

WHERE IN THE WORLD? 12

DAILY LIFE 14

A HUMPBACK WHALE'S LIFE 18

FAVORITE FOODS 22

BIRTH 24

DEVELOPMENT 26

FUTURE 28

FAST FACTS 30

GLOSSARY 31

ONLINE RESOURCES 31

INDEX 32

THE HUMPBACK WHALE

The world is full of awesome, powerful animals. Humpback whales (HUHMP-back WAYHLS) live along the ocean coasts. Many know them as super singers.

At certain times of the year, male humpbacks fill the oceans with moans, groans, and squeals. These songs can be heard from nearly 12 miles (20 km) away. No one is quite sure why humpbacks sing.

DID YOU KNOW?

Many humpbacks can sing together. However, each whale sings its own song.

While whales live in water, they breathe air. Whales breathe through the two blowholes on top of their heads.

BOLD BODIES

Humpback whales have bold bodies. They weigh 50,000 to 80,000 pounds (32,000 to 36,000 kg). And, they can be up to 60 feet (12 to 18 m) long. That is as long as a semitruck!

The humpback's body is black or dark gray. Each whale has different white markings on its front fins, **flukes**, and belly. It is easy to notice a whale by its unusual markings.

Adult female humpback whales are larger than the males.

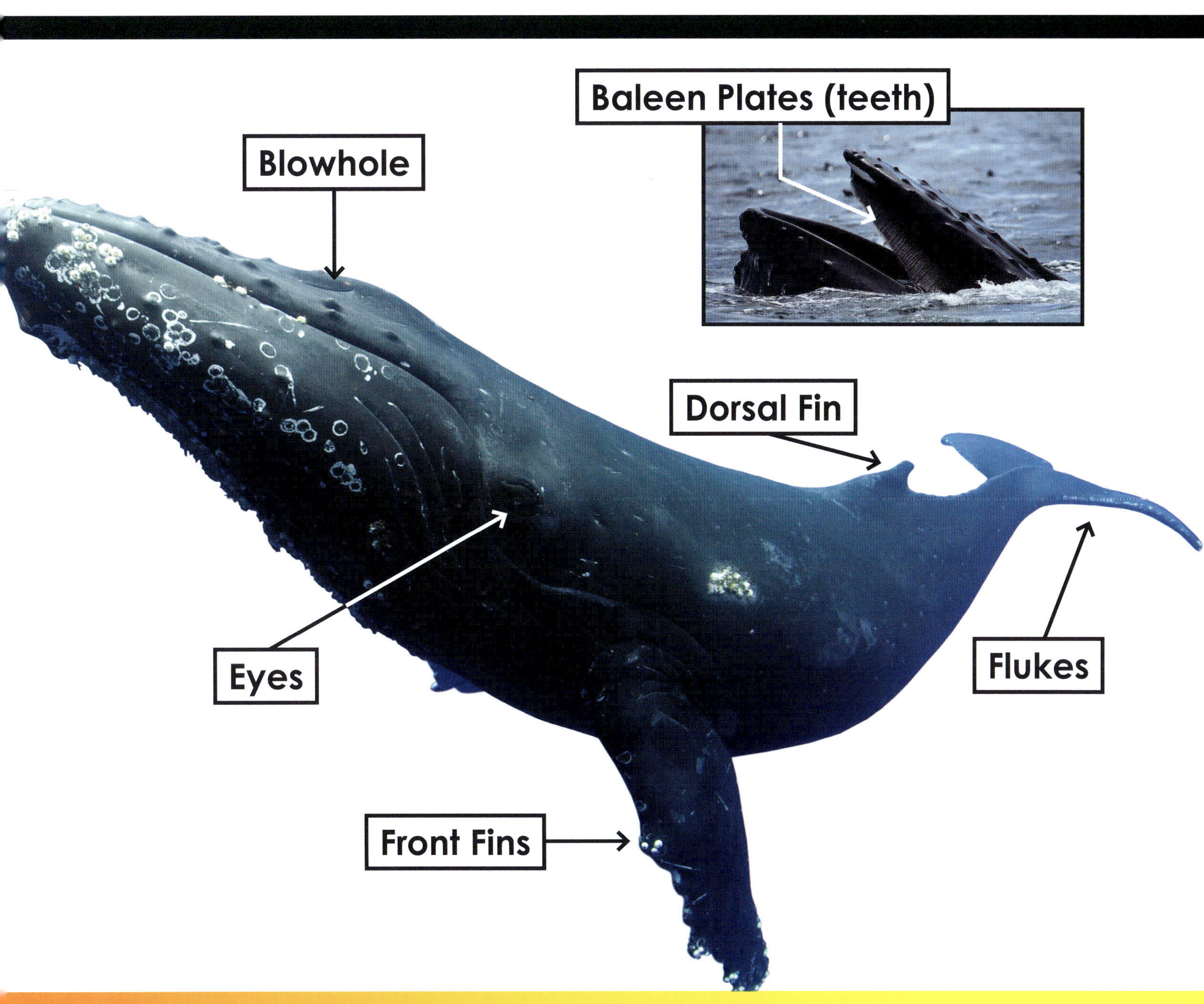
Baleen Plates (teeth)
Blowhole
Dorsal Fin
Eyes
Flukes
Front Fins

THAT'S AWESOME!

These whales are super singers. Both males and females make sounds. But only the males can produce an organized song.

Their moans, howls, cries, and other noises can last for hours. Many scientists think that whales sing to **communicate** with each other. Or they may sing to attract females.

Humpbacks sing by squeezing air bubbles near their blowholes. As the air moves, it makes sounds.

Humpbacks are the most **vocal** whales. Each group of whales has its own songs. Their songs can change from year to year. No one knows why the whales choose to sing new songs.

The humpback whale's song is the most advanced song in the whole animal kingdom.

WHERE IN THE

Humpback whales live along the coasts of all oceans. Many **migrate** between cooler feeding waters in summer and warmer **breeding** waters in winter.

These whales swim near the surface of the ocean. When not migrating, they like to swim in shallow waters.

WORLD?
= WHERE HUMPBACK WHALES LIVE
ARCTIC OCEAN
North America
Europe
Asia
PACIFIC OCEAN
NORTH ATLANTIC OCEAN
Africa
South America
PACIFIC OCEAN
INDIAN OCEAN
SOUTH ATLANTIC OCEAN
Australia
N
W
E
S

DAILY LIFE

Humpbacks are playful animals. They leap out of the water when they are happy. They also jump to **communicate** or to warn others of danger.

When a whale **breaches**, most of its body comes out of the water. Then it lands on its back or side. Some whales like to slap their tails against the water. This is called slapping or lob-tailing.

A layer of blubber keeps whales warm in cold water.

These **mammals** are called baleen whales. Baleen are thick hair-like plates in the upper jaw. Humpbacks use them to eat **plankton** and **krill** from the water.

Baleen whales take large amounts of water into their mouths. Then, they push the water out through the baleen. This strains the water so only food is left for them to swallow.

When humpbacks feel sad, they moan or whine. These noises are similar to how humans cry for the loss of a loved one.

A HUMPBACK WHALE'S LIFE

An adult humpback's dive usually lasts about 15 minutes. It can hold its breath for more than 45 minutes. And it can dive more than 650 feet (198 m) underwater.

These **mammals** are slow swimmers. They normally swim about three to nine miles (5 to 15 km) per hour. During feeding season, they slow down to about one to three miles (2 to 5 km) per hour.

DID YOU KNOW?

Humpbacks are peaceful animals. They are friendly to other whales, fish, and dolphins.

All whales have front flippers. Inside the flippers, the bones are shaped similar to human hands.

Humpback whales are always traveling. They travel at all times of day and night. Every year, they swim thousands of miles to their summer feeding grounds.

They travel in pods of two to 15 whales. These pods only stay together for a short amount of time.

Shelled animals called barnacles attach themselves to the skin of humpbacks. One whale can carry almost 1,000 pounds (450 kg) of barnacles!

FAVORITE FOODS

Whales spend a lot of time looking for food along the coastlines. They eat **krill**, **plankton**, and small fish.

When hunting, a whale will blow large bubbles to create a kind of net around its **prey**. Then the fish swim into the bubble. This way, the humpback can eat thousands of fish in one bite!

A humpback will eat about 5,500 pounds (2,500 kg) of food each day during feeding season.

BIRTH

A female humpback is **pregnant** for about 11 months. Then she gives birth to one calf. A calf is 13 to 15 feet (4 to 5 m) long. It weighs about 1,500 pounds (680 kg) at birth.

DID YOU KNOW?

A female can have a calf every two to four years.

Calves drink milk from their mothers. They drink up to 130 gallons (492 L) each day. Calves nurse for about six months.

DEVELOPMENT

Humpbacks begin **breeding** when they are between five and seven years old. However, they continue to grow until they are ten years old. In the wild, humpbacks live to be about 50 years old.

Mothers and calves swim close together. As they swim, their flippers often touch.

FUTURE

Humpback whales were taken off the list of **endangered** animals in 2016. Today, there are about 80,000 humpbacks in the world. That is only one-third of the original number.

Luckily, there are many people who work hard to save the humpback whales. Because of them, the number of whales continues to grow.

Over-fishing is hurting the humpback whales. Much of the humpbacks' food is caught in large nets that are meant to catch other fish.

FAST FACTS

ANIMAL TYPE: Mammal

SIZE: 39 to 62 feet (12 to 19 m)

WEIGHT: 80,000 pounds (36,300 kg)

HABITAT: Along costal regions

DIET: Krill, plankton, and small fish

AWESOME ANIMAL POWER:
Their beautiful songs are the most advanced tunes in the whole animal kingdom.

GLOSSARY

breach to jump or leap up out of the water.

breed to produce animals by mating.

communicate (kuh-MYOO-nuh-kayt) to give and receive information, such as knowledge or news.

endangered in danger of dying out.

fluke tail fins.

krill tiny floating sea animals that resemble shrimp and are a chief food source of some whales.

mammal a member of a group of living beings. Mammals make milk to feed their babies and usually have hair or fur on their skin.

migrate to move from one place to another to find food or have babies.

plankton tiny animals and plants that float in a body of water.

pregnant having one or more babies growing within the body.

prey an animal hunted or killed by a predator for food.

vocal uttered by the voice.

ONLINE RESOURCES

To learn more about humpback whales, visit **abdobooklinks.com**. These links are routinely monitored and updated to provide the most current information available.

INDEX

behavior **4, 5, 8, 10, 12, 14, 16, 17, 18, 19, 20, 22, 23, 27, 30**

birth **24**

climate **12, 15, 20**

communication **4, 5, 8, 9, 10, 11, 14, 17, 30**

conservation **28, 29**

development **24, 25, 26**

food **16, 18, 22, 23, 25, 29, 30**

habitat **4, 12, 22, 30**

homes **4, 12**

life span **26**

mating **12, 26**

migration **12, 18, 20**

physical characteristics **5, 6, 7, 8, 9, 15, 16, 18, 19, 21, 24, 25, 26, 30**

population **28**

sea creatures **16, 19, 21, 22, 29**